CHICAGO BEARS

MATT SCHEFF

Apex is distributed by North Star Editions:
sales@northstareditions.com | 888-417-0195

Produced for Apex by Red Line Editorial.

Photographs ©: Adrian Kraus/AP Images, cover, 1; Kamil Krzaczynski/AP Images, 4–5, 58–59; Michael Reaves/Getty Images Sport/Getty Images, 6–7; Kaufmann & Fabry Co./Library of Congress, 8–9; Bettmann/Getty Images, 10–11, 12–13, 14–15, 20–21, 22–23, 24–25, 50–51, 52–53; Sylvia Allen/Getty Images Sport/Getty Images, 16–17; Mitchell Layton/Getty Images Sport/Getty Images, 19; Focus On Sport/Getty Images Sport/Getty Images, 26–27; Peter Read Miller/AP Images, 29, 57; Jamie Squire/Getty Images Sport/Getty Images, 30–31; Jed Jacobsohn/Getty Images Sport/Getty Images, 32–33; Tom Hauck/Getty Images Sport/Getty Images, 34–35; Thearon W. Henderson/Getty Images Sport/Getty Images, 36–37; David Banks/Getty Images Sport/Getty Images, 38–39; Jonathan Daniel/Getty Images Sport/Getty Images, 40–41, 42–43, 54–55; Gregory Shamus/Getty Images Sport/Getty Images, 44–45; Otto Greule Jr/Getty Images Sport/Getty Images, 47; AP Images, 48–49

Library of Congress Control Number: 2023921990

ISBN
979-8-89250-150-7 (hardcover)
979-8-89250-167-5 (paperback)
979-8-89250-291-7 (ebook pdf)
979-8-89250-184-2 (hosted ebook)

Printed in the United States of America
Mankato, MN
012025

NOTE TO PARENTS AND EDUCATORS

Apex books are designed to build literacy skills in striving readers. Exciting, high-interest content attracts and holds readers' attention. The text is carefully leveled to allow students to achieve success quickly.

TABLE OF CONTENTS

CHAPTER 1

MONSTERS OF THE MIDWAY

A cold wind blows across Soldier Field. The Chicago Bears make a big play. Thousands of fans cheer. The Bears are known as the "Monsters of the Midway." The nickname honors the team's toughness.

Soldier Field can seat more than 60,000 fans.

It's late in the game. The Bears need to score. Their quarterback takes the snap. The defense rushes in. Wide receiver D. J. Moore gets open deep. The quarterback throws the ball. Moore catches it in the end zone. It's a touchdown for Chicago! The fans roar.

SOLDIER FIELD

Soldier Field was built in 1924. But the Bears did not start playing there until 1971. The stadium stands near Lake Michigan. Breezes often come in off the lake. That helps make Soldier Field the NFL's windiest stadium.

D. J. Moore catches a touchdown pass during a 2023 game.

CHAPTER 2

EARLY HISTORY

In 1919, a new football team formed in Decatur, Illinois. The team was called the Staleys. In 1920, the Staleys helped create the NFL. They also began playing in Chicago that year. The move paid off quickly. The Staleys won the NFL title in 1921.

In 1920, about 2.7 million people lived in Chicago, Illinois.

In 1922, the Staleys changed their name. They became the Chicago Bears. The Bears won NFL titles in 1932 and 1933. Then they shined in the 1940s. They won four titles that decade. In 1942, the team was almost perfect. The Bears went 11–0 in the regular season. But Washington beat them in the title game.

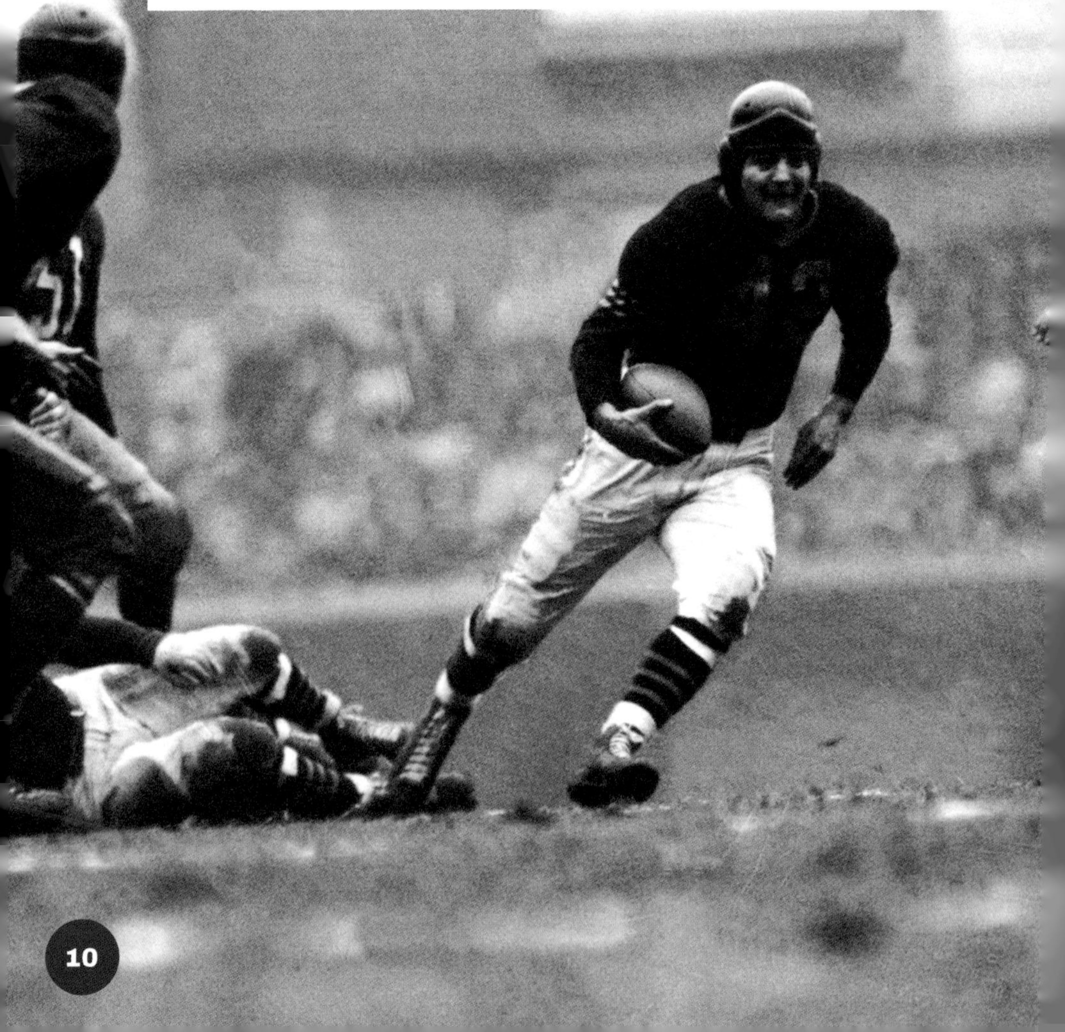

PLAYER, COACH, OWNER

George Halas joined the Staleys in 1920. He was both a player and a coach. The next year, he became the team's owner, too. Halas stopped playing after the 1929 season. But he spent many more years coaching. His final game was in 1967.

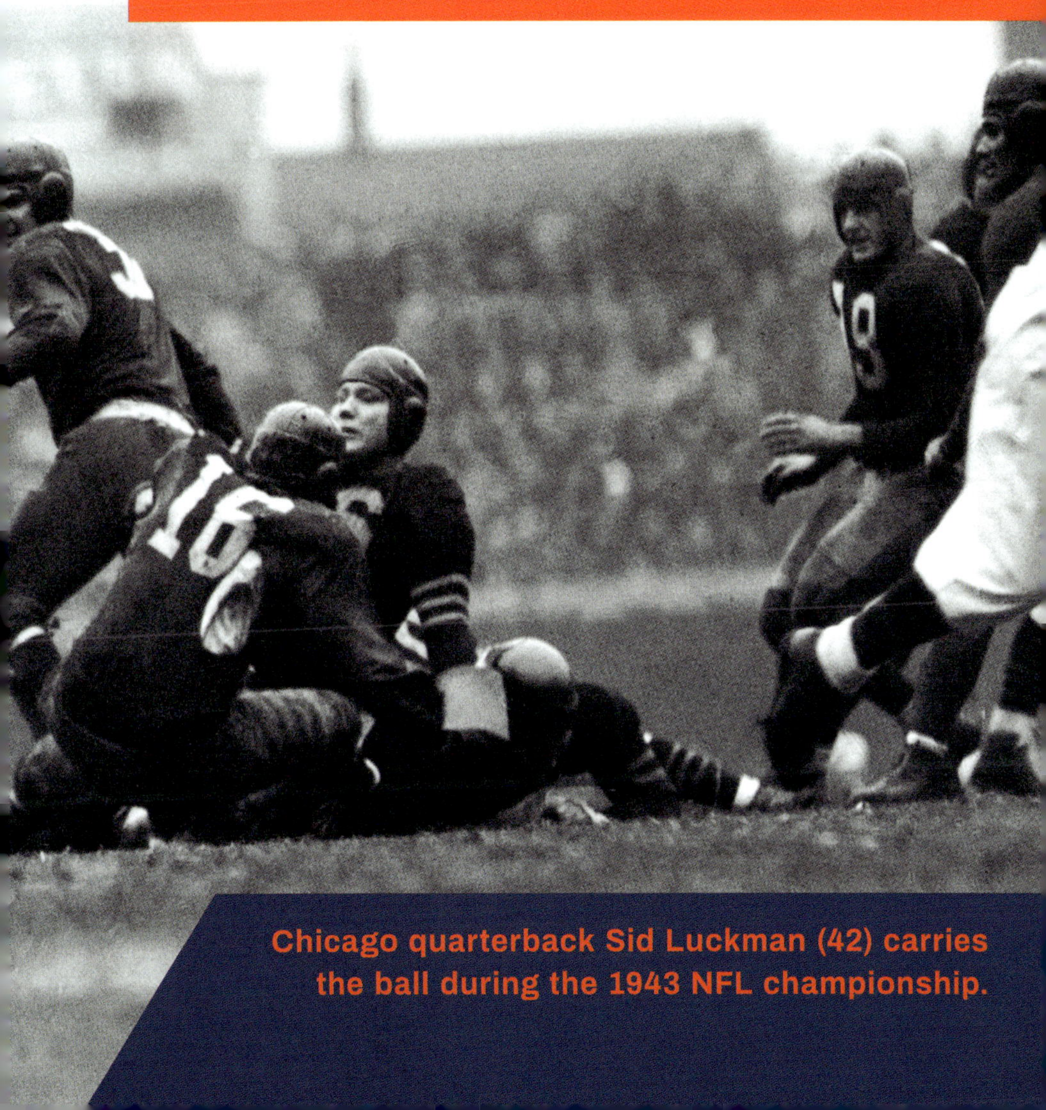

Chicago quarterback Sid Luckman (42) carries the ball during the 1943 NFL championship.

Chicago reached the championship just once in the 1950s. The team lost to the New York Giants in 1956. But the Bears got another shot in 1963. Coach George Halas led them to an 11–1–2 season. They faced the Giants again in the title game. They used a crushing defense to win 14–10.

THE 1963 DEFENSE

The 1963 Giants led the league offensively. But the Bears' defense shut them down in the title game. Defenders nabbed five interceptions. The Bears also used a new zone defense. That completely fooled New York.

Bears defenders take down the New York Giants' quarterback during the 1963 title game.

Mike Ditka coaches the Bears players during a 1984 game.

The Bears hit rough times after their 1963 title. Chicago didn't win another playoff game for more than two decades. But things turned around in the 1980s. Mike Ditka became head coach. He led the Bears to the conference title game in 1984. They lost. But the Bears were on the rise.

The 1985 team brought Chicago back to glory. In the playoffs, the Bears first beat the Giants. Then they took down the Los Angeles Rams. Chicago didn't allow a single point in either game. These shutouts took the Bears to the Super Bowl. They crushed the New England Patriots 46–10. It was Chicago's first Super Bowl title.

THE SUPER BOWL SHUFFLE

The 1985 Bears made a song called "The Super Bowl Shuffle." Players sang and danced in the popular music video. The song was even up for a Grammy Award.

Bears defenders sack the New England Patriots' quarterback during the Super Bowl.

COACH SPOTLIGHT

MIKE DITKA

Mike Ditka started his NFL career in 1961. He played tight end. Back then, it was mostly a blocking position. Ditka was a great blocker. But he also helped change the position. He used his great hands to become a skilled receiver. Ditka played a key part in Chicago's 1963 championship team. He also made five straight Pro Bowls as a Bear.

In 1982, Ditka became Chicago's head coach. His tough style and fiery energy kicked the Bears into high gear. Three years later, he led the Bears to a Super Bowl title.

DITKA WAS NAMED NFL COACH OF THE YEAR TWICE.

BEARS

CHAPTER 3

LEGENDS

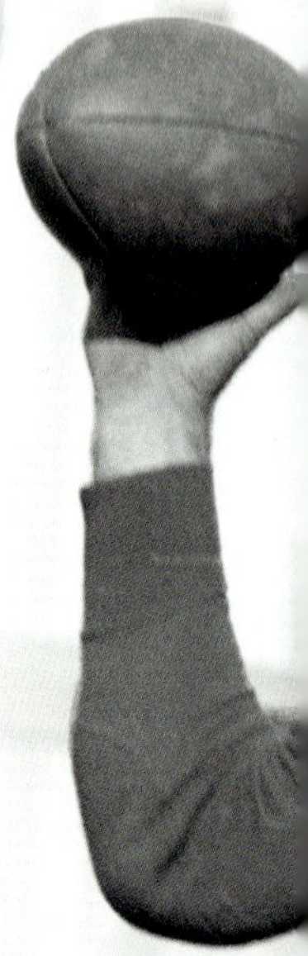

Some of the NFL's first stars played for the Bears. Bronko Nagurski was pure power. As a running back, he rolled over defenders. He also threw passes. Nagurski played defense, too. He was a star linebacker for the Bears.

Bronko Nagurski played for the Bears from 1930 to 1937 and in 1943.

Sid Luckman led the Bears to four NFL titles.

Quarterback Sid Luckman formed the heart of the powerful 1940s Bears. He led a strong passing game. He often threw to end Ken Kavanaugh. He also passed to running back Ray McLean. Like Nagurski, Luckman played more than one position. He also served as the team's punter and defensive back.

THE T FORMATION

Luckman ran an offense called the T formation. Three running backs lined up behind him. Defenses wondered where everyone was going. That created huge openings and big gains.

Gale Sayers returns a kickoff for a 96-yard touchdown during a 1965 game.

Gale Sayers played in only 68 NFL games. Injuries cut his career short. But the running back made his mark. Sayers amazed fans with his speed. He became known as the "Kansas Comet." In 1965, Sayers scored six touchdowns in one game. Going into 2024, that was still tied for the NFL record.

HARD HITTER

Linebacker Dick Butkus joined the Bears in 1965. He hammered offenses. Butkus twice earned the Defensive Player of the Year Award.

Mike Singletary closes in on the Tampa Bay Buccaneers' quarterback during a 1988 game.

Many football experts say the 1985 Bears' defense was the best ever. Linebacker Mike Singletary led the way. He tackled often, and he tackled hard. Singletary was named the Defensive Player of the Year in 1985 and 1988.

Richard Dent was another superstar. The defensive end knew how to find the quarterback. In 1985, Dent led the league with 17 sacks.

PLAYER SPOTLIGHT

WALTER PAYTON

Running back Walter Payton stood just 5-foot-10 (178 cm). He weighed 200 pounds (91 kg). But his quickness made him hard to tackle. As a result, he became one of the greatest running backs in history.

Payton's best year came in 1977. He won the NFL rushing title. He was named Most Valuable Player (MVP), too. Payton helped the 1985 Bears win the Super Bowl. Then he retired after the 1987 season. At the time, he was the NFL's all-time leading rusher. The record stood for nearly 20 years.

WALTER PAYTON'S MOVES EARNED HIM THE NICKNAME "SWEETNESS."

34

CHAPTER 4

RECENT HISTORY

The Bears struggled through most of the 1990s and early 2000s. In 2004, they hired Lovie Smith as head coach. Smith helped turn the team around. The Bears won their division in 2005. They were even better in 2006. A strong defense helped Chicago go 13–3.

In January 2007, the Bears beat the New Orleans Saints 39–14 to advance to the Super Bowl.

Devin Hester's kickoff-return touchdown in the Super Bowl went for 92 yards.

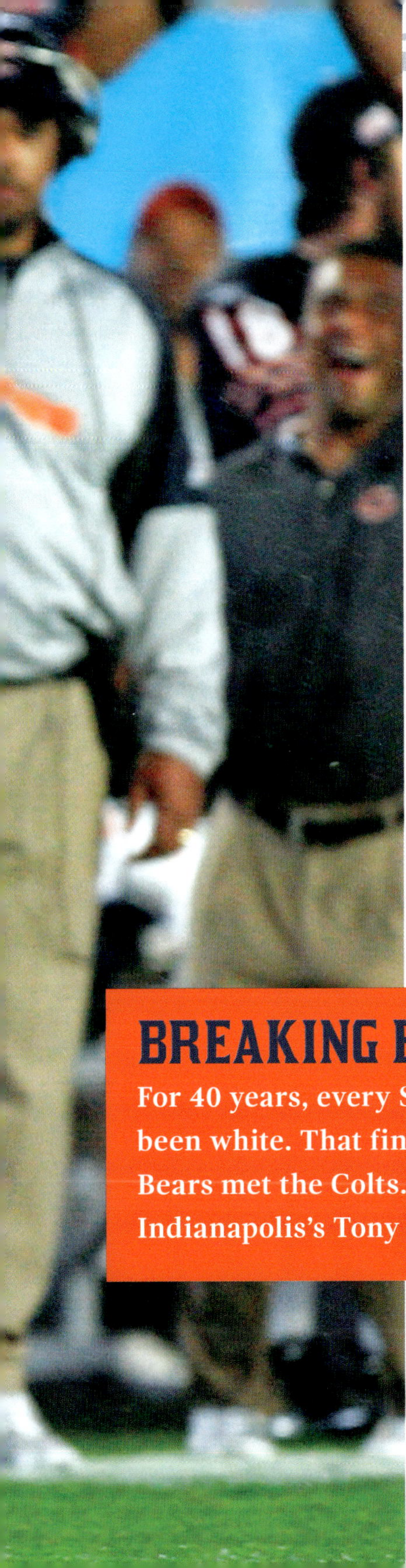

The 2006 Bears made it all the way to the Super Bowl. It was their first trip since 1985. They faced the Indianapolis Colts. Devin Hester returned the opening kickoff for a Bears touchdown. But it was all downhill from there. The Colts won 29–17.

BREAKING BARRIERS

For 40 years, every Super Bowl head coach had been white. That finally changed when the Bears met the Colts. Chicago's Lovie Smith and Indianapolis's Tony Dungy were both Black.

In 2010, the Bears won the division again. They reached the conference championship game. The Bears faced their biggest rival, the Green Bay Packers. However, Chicago quarterback Jay Cutler got hurt early. The Bears almost came back in the fourth quarter. But Green Bay held on to win.

A NEW OLD STADIUM

Soldier Field is more than 100 years old. In 2002, the team updated the stadium. Builders kept the famous stone columns outside. But they gave Soldier Field a new inside. The upgrades helped. Still, some fans thought the Bears needed a new, modern stadium.

Jay Cutler (6) hands the ball to Matt Forte (22) during the conference title game of the 2010 season.

For most of the 2010s, Bears fans had little to celebrate. The team went 12–4 in 2018. But Chicago lost in the first round of the playoffs. However, Matt Eberflus took over as head coach in 2022. And the Bears were building a core of young talent. Fans hoped for a bright future.

Allen Robinson makes a diving catch during a 2018 game against the San Francisco 49ers.

CHAPTER 5

MODERN STARS

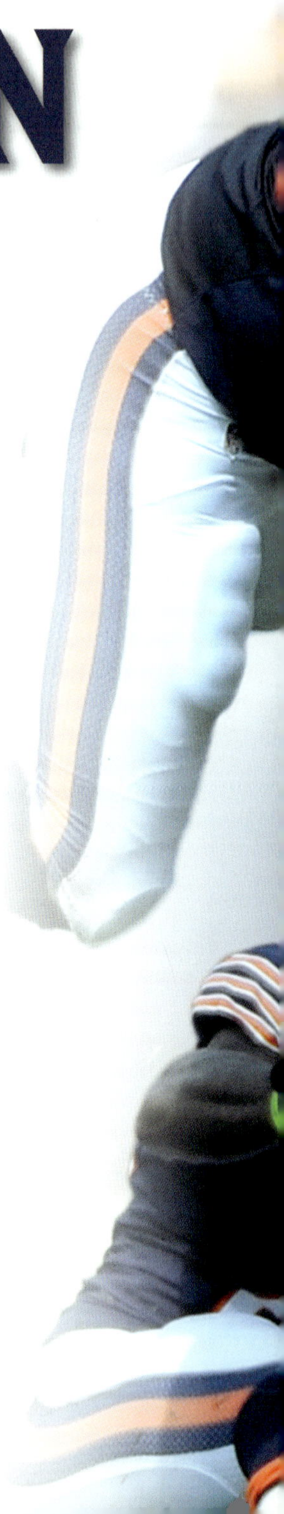

Brian Urlacher led the Bears' defense in the 2000s. He made life tough for offenses. Fellow linebacker Lance Briggs helped, too. Briggs made seven straight Pro Bowls. Charles Tillman was a star cornerback. He forced fumbles with ease.

Lance Briggs tackles a Cincinnati Bengal during a 2013 game.

Devin Hester runs with the ball during a 2008 game.

Devin Hester was one of a kind. He played wide receiver. But he was best known for returning punts and kicks. Many call him the best return man in NFL history. Hester returned 14 punts for touchdowns. That set an NFL record. Hester also scored five kick-return touchdowns.

OLD RIVALS

The Bears and Packers share the oldest rivalry in pro football. Going into 2024, the teams had met 208 times. Unfortunately for Bears fans, the Packers had won more games.

Matt Forte recorded nearly 2,000 rushing and receiving yards in 2013.

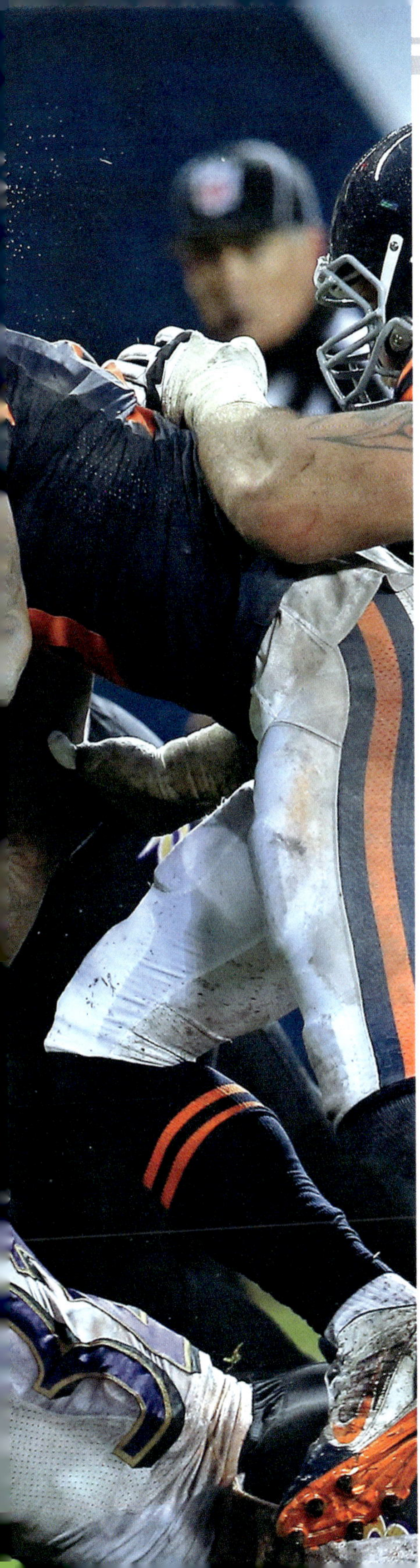

The Bears struggled in the 2010s. But they had plenty of stars. Running back Matt Forte was a strong rusher. He was a skilled pass catcher, too. Quarterback Jay Cutler threw like a cannon. And Robbie Gould kicked steady even at windy Soldier Field.

In the early 2020s, new stars gave Bears fans hope. Tight end Cole Kmet joined in 2020. The Bears got receiver D. J. Moore in a trade. He quickly became a top target. On defense, the Bears added Montez Sweat in 2023. In 2024, they selected quarterback Caleb Williams No. 1 overall in the draft.

LINEBACKER DUO

From 2018 to 2021, the Bears featured two elite linebackers. Khalil Mack racked up sack after sack. Roquan Smith was a rising star. He used his speed to cover the entire field.

Caption: Caleb Williams (left) celebrates being picked No. 1 overall in April 2024.

BRIAN URLACHER

The Bears have long been known for great linebackers. In the 2000s, Brian Urlacher stepped up as the latest star. Urlacher made his name stopping passes. He used his strength and speed against blockers. He also used his smarts to read offenses. That way, he knew exactly where to go.

Urlacher played for 13 seasons. All of them were with the Bears. He made eight Pro Bowls during that time. He also racked up more than 1,300 tackles. In 2005, Urlacher was the NFL Defensive Player of the Year.

BRIAN URLACHER ENTERED THE PRO FOOTBALL HALL OF FAME IN 2018.

Riddell
54
C
54

CHAPTER 6

TEAM TRIVIA

In the 1920s, some NFL players did not wear helmets. But by the late 1930s, almost all did. Bears end Dick Plasman held out. He was the last player to go without one. His final game without a helmet came in the 1940s.

Dick Plasman (14) poses with the title-winning 1942 Bears.

Bill Osmanski (9) scored the Bears' first touchdown of their 73–0 win.

The Bears faced Washington in the 1940 NFL Championship Game. It was a blowout. The Bears were unstoppable. They won 73–0. It remains the largest margin of victory in NFL history. And it happened in the biggest game of the year.

IN THE FAMILY

George Halas bought the Bears in 1921. He owned the team until his death in 1983. Then his oldest daughter, Virginia Halas McCaskey, became the owner. She turned 100 years old in 2023. She had owned the Bears for 40 years.

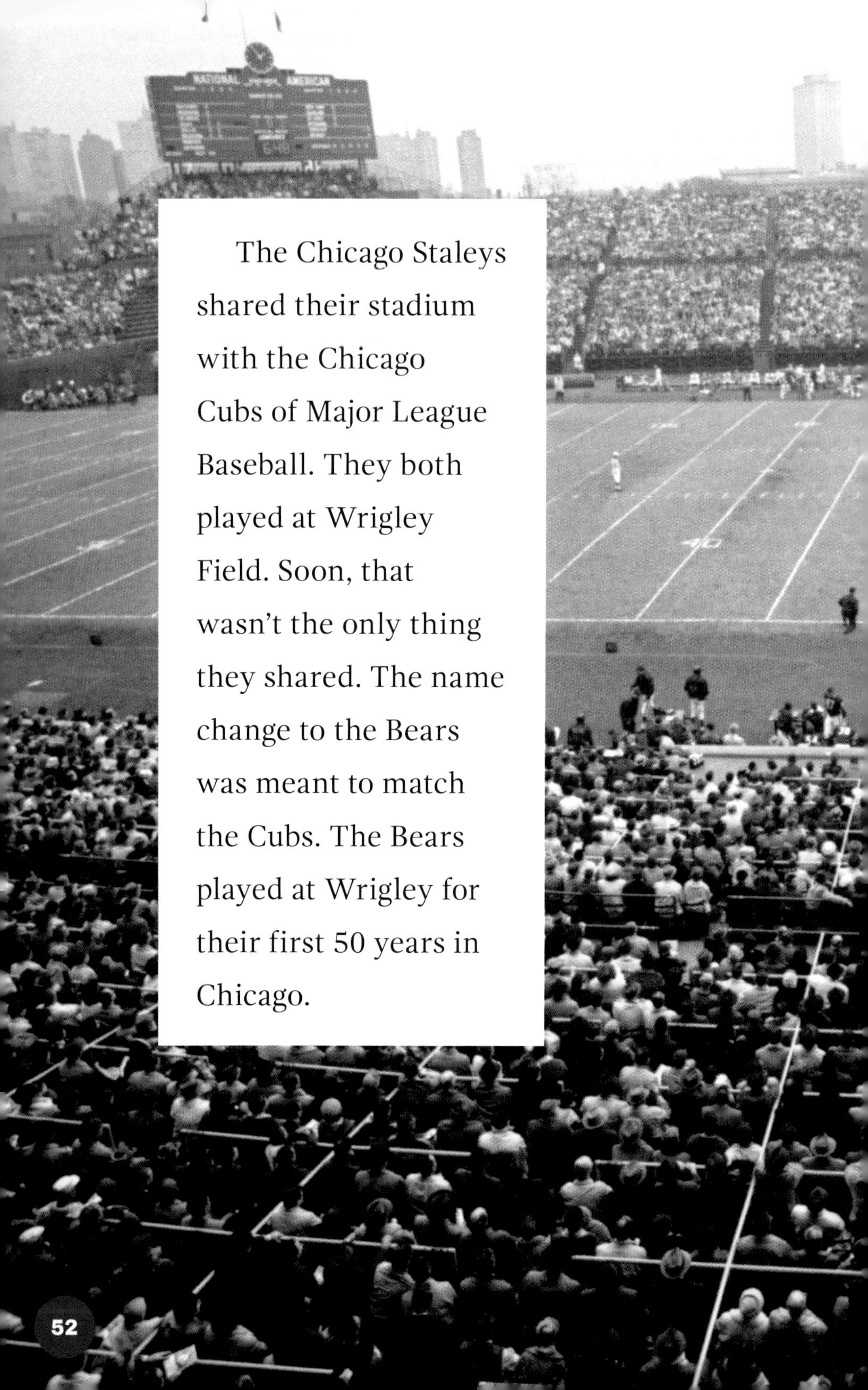

The Chicago Staleys shared their stadium with the Chicago Cubs of Major League Baseball. They both played at Wrigley Field. Soon, that wasn't the only thing they shared. The name change to the Bears was meant to match the Cubs. The Bears played at Wrigley for their first 50 years in Chicago.

Fans attend a 1961 game at Wrigley Field between the Bears and the Los Angeles Rams.

Defensive tackle Steve McMichael entered the Pro Football Hall of Fame in 2024.

The Bears have more players in the Pro Football Hall of Fame than any other team. As of 2024, Chicago had 32. The Packers were second. They had 28 Hall of Fame players.

CROSSTOWN RIVALS

The Bears weren't always the only NFL team in town. The Chicago Cardinals were also one of the NFL's first teams. The Cardinals moved to St. Louis in 1960. In 1987, they moved to Arizona.

TEAM RECORDS

All-Time Passing Yards: 23,443
Jay Cutler (2009–16)

All-Time Touchdown Passes: 154
Jay Cutler (2009–16)

All-Time Rushing Yards: 16,726
Walter Payton (1975–87)

All-Time Receiving Yards: 5,059
Johnny Morris (1958–67)

All-Time Interceptions: 38
Gary Fencik (1976–87)

All-Time Sacks: 124.5
Richard Dent (1983–93, 1995)

All-Time Scoring: 1,207
Robbie Gould (2005–15)

All-Time Coaching Wins: 318
George Halas (1920–29, 1933–42, 1946–55, 1958–67)

NFL Titles: 8
(1921, 1932, 1933, 1940, 1941, 1943, 1946, 1963)

Super Bowl Titles: 1
(1985)

All statistics are accurate through 2023.

COMPREHENSION QUESTIONS

Write your answers on a separate piece of paper.

1. Write a paragraph that explains the main ideas of Chapter 4.

2. Who do you think was the greatest player in Chicago Bears history? Why?

3. Who is the main rival of the Bears?

   A. Indianapolis Colts
   B. New York Giants
   C. Green Bay Packers

4. What was the biggest reason the Bears won the Super Bowl in 1985?

   A. strong defense
   B. strong special teams
   C. mistakes by the other team

5. What does **shutouts** mean in this book?

Chicago didn't allow a single point in either game. These ***shutouts*** *took the Bears to the Super Bowl.*

A. games in which the opponent wins easily

B. games in which the opponent doesn't score

C. games in which the opponent reaches the Super Bowl

6. What does **elite** mean in this book?

From 2018 to 2021, the Bears featured two ***elite*** *linebackers. Khalil Mack racked up sack after sack. Roquan Smith was a rising star.*

A. not important

B. among the best

C. very weak

Answer key on page 64.

GLOSSARY

conference
A group of teams that make up part of a sports league.

division
In the NFL, a group of teams that make up part of a conference.

formation
The positions where players line up before a play begins.

interceptions
Passes that are caught by a defensive player.

margin of victory
The difference in points between the winner and loser of a game.

retired
Ended one's career.

rival
The opponent that a team has the most intense competition against.

sacks
Plays that happen when a defender tackles the quarterback before he can throw the ball.

snap
The start of each play when the center passes the ball back to the quarterback.

zone defense
A type of defense in which players cover areas instead of individuals.

TO LEARN MORE

BOOKS

Adamson, Thomas. *The Chicago Bears.* Minneapolis: Bellwether Media, 2024.

Levit, Joe. *G.O.A.T. Football Teams.* Minneapolis: Lerner Publications, 2021.

Streeter, Anthony. *Super Bowl All-Time Greats.* Mendota Heights, MN: Press Box Books, 2025.

ONLINE RESOURCES

Visit **www.apexeditions.com** to find links and resources related to this title.

ABOUT THE AUTHOR

Matt Scheff is an author and artist living in Alaska. He enjoys mountain climbing, fishing, and curling up with his two Siberian huskies to watch sports.

INDEX

ANSWER KEY:

1. Answers will vary; 2. Answers will vary; 3. C; 4. A; 5. B; 6. B